ECO–DISASTERS

John Hamilton

Published by Abdo & Daughters, 4940 Viking Drive Suite 622, Edina, Minnesota 55435.

Library bound edition distributed by Rockbottom Books, Pentagon Tower, P.O. Box 36036, Minneapolis, Minnesota 55435.

Cover Photo by: Stockmarket
Inside Photos by: The Bettmann Archive, Peter Arnold, Inc., AP\Wide World Photos, Archive Photos.

Edited By: Sue L. Hamilton

LIBRARY OF CONGRESS CATALOGING-IN-PUBLICATION DATA

Hamilton, John, 1959 -
  Eco-disasters / written by John Hamilton.
     p.   cm. -- (Target Earth)
  Includes bibliographical references and index.
  Summary: Presents brief accounts of six environmental disasters including the Exxon Valdez oil spill, the Chernobyl nuclear power plant accident, and the oil field fires in Kuwait.
  ISBN 1-56239-200-X
  1. Environmental degradation -- Juvenile literature. [1. Environmental degradation 2. Man -- Influence on nature. 3. Pollution.] I. Title.   II. Series.
  GE140.5.H36   1993
  363.7 -- dc20
  [B]   93-10259
                                                             CIP
                                                             AC

All Target Earth™ Earthmobile books are hardcover with full–color illustrations & photographs, and manufactured with environmentally safe products. The reinforced library binding is guaranteed for the life of the book.

Thanks To The Trees From Which This Recycled Paper Was First Made.

Table of Contents

Chapter 1

The *Amoco Cadiz* Oil Spill

**Journal of Jacques Rochelle, Reporter
(April 10, 1978)**

As I write this, my hands shake. Just got off the helicopter from Paris. The pilot took me directly to the wreck for an overhead view before we landed. The supertanker *Amoco Cadiz* lies just off the Brittany Coast in northwest France. Cracked in two like an egg after smashing on the rocks, the ship bobs in the rough water. To me it looks like an ugly black carcass floating on the waves. I'm told that at least 68 million gallons (257 million liters) of crude oil spilled into the sea. 68 million gallons(257 million liters)! The size of this disaster is incredible; it is the worst oil spill in history. Madness!

The oil spreads across the water like an ugly black hand, smothering the life out of everything it touches. So far we've found 25 kinds of dead fish washed up on shore. Thousands of birds lie on the black beaches, dead or writhing in agony, waiting for death. This coastline used to be untouched. Beds of seaweed just offshore are usually harvested to make drugs and fertilizer. Now they are wiped out. Driven by the high winds, the oil slick has oozed from the American-owned tanker and polluted more than 100 miles (160 km) of this beautiful shoreline. From the air it looks like a huge, ugly dark tide.

The supertanker Amoco Cadiz *lies crippled and gushing oil off France's Brittany Coast in 1978.*

Officials from the government seem helpless to stop the slick. Winds have howled so fiercely this week that floating plastic barricades have failed to contain the oil. They are afraid to use detergents to clean the oil for fear of hurting marine life. Fishermen work day and night to move oysters and scallops out of harm's way. It seems useless, but we must do something.

I'm afraid it will be many years before this coastline recovers, if ever.

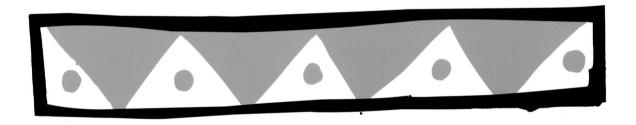

Postscript: *The spill from the* Amoco Cadiz *was the worst the world has ever seen. After 15 years the recovery of the ecosystem along 200 miles (320 km) of France's Brittany Coast is still not complete. The disaster heightened our awareness of how a single spill can have devastating effects on our fragile coastlines. The growing use of "supertankers" to transport oil only heightens the danger.*

Chapter 2

Chernobyl Nuclear Disaster

Diary of Leonid Legasov, age 11
(April 26, 1986; 1:30 A.M.)

I woke up in the middle of the night to the sound of explosions. I was in my bed in the small town of Pripyat, Ukraine. Looking out my window, I could see flames leaping into the night sky. It looked like the fire was coming from the Chernobyl nuclear power plant. Sirens screamed as fire trucks raced toward the plant. Mother and Father woke up, looking scared, making me scared. Everybody is screaming and shouting. What is going on?

(7:00 A.M.)
The Army loaded everybody in the village into big trucks. We're leaving forever. There's been a bad accident at Chernobyl. I don't understand why we have to leave. Everything looks okay. We're just farmers. We haven't done anything wrong. Father says radiation is floating everywhere, invisible deadly dust that makes everything sick or die. The Army won't let me take my dog, Lessy. No animals, they said, not even pets. How will she survive? Where will we go? Has the radiation already harmed us?

As our Army truck sped out of town, an ambulance passed us, heading for Kiev. As it passed, I looked inside and saw a man in back, his shirt off. His skin was all blistered and red, hanging off him like torn curtains. He was throwing up. My father said he must have been a fireman fighting the blaze at the power plant.

The soldier driving the truck told me everyone within 30 kilometers (19 miles) of the plant is being evacuated. Where will we go? As we speed away, I glance back and see our house in the distance. Lessy barks like crazy, tugging at her chain in the front yard. I am afraid.

Journal of Nils Trom, Swedish Nuclear Engineer (April 28, 1986)

Our first warning in Sweden came at the Forsmark Nuclear Power Plant, just north of my home city of Stockholm. At 9:00 A.M. the plant's sensors warned of very high levels of radiation. Suspecting serious trouble, workers looked for a leak, but could find nothing. Outside, radiation readings taken from the ground and plants were showing levels five times normal. Something was horribly wrong. A gentle spring rain was falling, but it was rain containing deadly radiation. Stations in Finland, Norway and Denmark began reporting the same readings. But where was the radiation coming from?

The burned-out Chernobyl power plant's Reactor Four after the April 26, 1986, nuclear accident. The reactor has since been sealed in concrete.

(April 28, 1986; 9:00 P.M.)

Just watched a news report that finally answered the radiation mystery. All day the world suspected the source to be somewhere inside the Soviet Union, but the Russians said it wasn't true. Finally, on Moscow television, an announcer came on and made a brief announcement: "An accident has taken place at the Chernobyl power station, and one of the reactors was damaged. Measures are being taken to eliminate the consequences of the accident. Those affected by it are being given assistance. A government commission has been set up." That was the end of the official announcement. Incredible! How could they not give more details when so many lives are at risk?

All across Europe there is panic. Children and pregnant women stay inside. Fresh food and milk shipments are stopped when authorities find too much radiation.

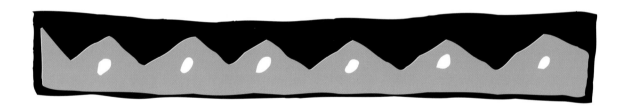

**Journal of Dimitre Omsk,
Construction Engineer
(November 1986)**

Seven months have passed since the worst nuclear accident ever. Chernobyl is now a safe place, though I would not care to live here. After one of the most frantic and massive construction projects in history, the stricken reactor lies inside a huge, black concrete tomb, sealed away for hundreds of years. The soil in the area has been sprayed with a plastic film and scraped by bulldozers, then sealed inside storage drums. Leaves from the trees have been buried, and crops and livestock destroyed.

New towns will be built, the old ones unlivable because of the radioactive contamination. Of the 116,000 people evacuated from the land around Chernobyl, 24,000 received a serious dose of radiation. Several hundred will die of cancer. In the Western Soviet Union and the rest of Europe, some say 5,000 people will die of cancer caused by the disaster. Others say 75,000. We may never know for sure.

Postscript: *After one of the most massive construction projects in history, the Chernobyl reactor and the area surrounding it are now "safe," with radiation levels even lower than permissible values. The stricken reactor lies entombed in concrete, where it must remain for hundreds of years. After the disaster, the Soviet government decided to halt construction of the types of dangerous, outdated reactors the Chernobyl power plant was based on. Also, a new emphasis on worker training and safety has been put in place. However, existing reactors of this same type are still running, and the various countries that now make up the former Soviet Union are still heavily dependent on nuclear power.*

Chapter 3

The *Exxon Valdez* Oil Spill

**Diary of Meriwa Lightfeather, age 12
(Saturday, March 25, 1989)**

Tonight is not a good night. Father walks around the house with a blank look on his face. I think he's still in shock from the trip in the fishing boat this morning. Since it's Saturday, I went along to help. Now I wish I had not. It was like sailing on a black, disgusting, smelly tide of goo. Dead birds and otters litter the shore. Father says there'll be no fishing this year. What are we supposed to do?

The *Exxon Valdez* oil spill happened in the worst place at the worst time. Prince William Sound, the area in Alaska where the ship ran aground, and where I live, is full of rocky coves and inlets. Spilled oil can collect in these places and stay for weeks or months. My village is in one such cove. If the oil comes here, it will kill all the young fish that spawn in the shallow water. Soon the birds will be coming back from their winter homes to nest.

The people in my village have been supportive of the oil industry in Alaska. It has brought prosperity, and nothing very bad has happened in many years.

But no more. Now we see how just one accident can ruin our lives. My father is a fisherman; that's all he knows. This year's spawn is wiped out by the toxic oil. Exxon says it will hire as many boats as possible to help clean up the spill, so father may yet work this year. But what about next year? If there are no fish, what will happen to us then?

Ship's Log, Captain Frank Whitten, U.S. Coast Guard (April 3, 1989)

The winds have picked up again. The waves should help break up the oil. This is good, but unfortunately it also means we won't be able to boom and skim the oil with our boats. Today we tried setting the oil on fire with laser beams, but it only worked in small patches. What a mess. It's taking too long to get the right equipment up here! The oil companies were supposed to be ready for such an emergency. If we learn anything from this tragedy, I hope it's the fact that accidents eventually will happen. We can't let ourselves think they won't, and then be caught unprepared when the unthinkable happens.

What happens next nobody can say for sure. This has now become the biggest oil spill in U.S. history, but more importantly, the biggest in a body of enclosed cold water. Prince William Sound doesn't have a lot of waves and currents and winds that would normally break up a big oil spill. How long will the oil hang around? Hard to tell, but I expect cleanup crews to be at work for a few years at least. Even so, after spilling over 10 million gallons (160 km) of crude oil, the *Exxon Valdez* will leave her mark on these beautiful waters for years to come. We expect that catches of salmon, herring, shrimp and crab will be ruined for several seasons.

Exxon Valdez oil tanker

Tugs pull the crippled tanker Exxon Valdez *after the supertanker ran aground in Alaska's Prince William Sound.*

Exxon has promised to clean up the spill and leave the area "the way it was before." I doubt this is possible. Even with all the skimmers recovering oil off the top of the water, we can't possibly get it all. In fact, we can only recover a fraction of what was spilled. Nature will do most of the cleanup, but it will take many years.

As I look back on this disaster, I see now more than ever the tug of war between our wish for an unspoiled environment and the demand for cheap energy. We can't have it both ways, yet we can't turn back time. Safety measures must be enforced. Other sources of energy must be put to use.

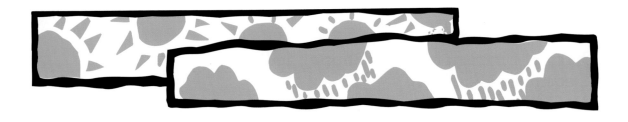

Postscript: *After four years of nature's cleaning action (the tides, wind and waves), plus hundreds of millions of dollars spent by the Exxon Corporation for the cleanup, Prince William Sound is slowing getting back to normal. If one digs below the surface on some beaches, though, traces of oil still can be found. Because of the spill, many new oil tankers are now being fitted with "double hulls." In theory, if a ship runs aground, only the outer hull will be damaged; the inner hull keeps the oil cargo safely contained. In theory. Nobody, though, truly believes that technology alone can keep future oil spills from occurring. Ultimately, it is our dependence on oil that is the cause of these spills.*

Chapter 4

Bhopal Toxic Cloud

Diary of Chandra Madras, Bhopal, India (December 17, 1984)

My mother and father are farmers on the edge of Bhopal, an industrial town. We live close to the Union Carbide pesticide plant. I don't know why they let a factory that uses poison gas to be so close to land where people live. They could have built farther away, perhaps in the jungle. Now it is too late, and we must bury our dead.

Last night around midnight, I woke up. I heard our cows making noises. I put on my clothes and went outside. I saw cows lying dead on the ground. As I watched, one cow came out of the night mist toward me. It groaned and fell down dead in front of me. Then my eyes started to sting. Something was terribly wrong. Tears streamed down my face. I could hardly breathe. I thought there was a plague. I ran back toward the house, to warn mother and father. I gasped for air. Then everything went black.

When I awoke, I was in the hospital, from where I write this. The doctors tell me poison gas escaped from the pesticide plant because of a faulty valve. A huge cloud, a misty fog of death, drifted over the slums next to the plant, killing hundreds as they slept. Then the cloud moved into the city. With no breeze to scatter the gas, the poison crept in silently, killing and injuring everyone in its path.

I'm told a policeman found me lying on the street. He carried me away to safety. Though my vision is still blurry, they say I will get my eyesight back. I was a lucky one. Mother and father died in the house. I do not know where my brothers and sisters are. Outside I can hear funeral processions marching down the street, more corpses to be burned at the Chhola Vishram cremation site. They tell me there are so many bodies lying in the streets, both people and animals, that the army is now helping to take them away before plague sets in. I hear dogs outside fighting for meat.

I have no family left. I am an orphan because of this disaster. What will happen to me now? Does anybody care?

*Two men carry blinded children to a hospital after poisonous gas escaped
from a storage tank at a pesticide factory in Bhopal, India, in 1984.*

Postscript: On the night of December 17, 1984, the world's worst industrial accident happened when 45 tons (40 thousand kg) of poison gas leaked from a Union Carbide pesticide plant in Bhopal, India. The deadly cloud killed more than 3,400 people, injuring 200,000, and killing countless animals. The government of India charged Union Carbide with carelessness, and charged company chief Warren Anderson with murder. The government also demanded $3.3 billion to pay victims of the accident.

More than four years after the accident, India's Supreme Court announced a settlement of all claims against Union Carbide. The company will pay $470 million, to be distributed to the victims by a special commission. In exchange, India will drop criminal charges against Union Carbide and its officers. The lawyer representing India said, "It's a fair and adequate settlement for the victims."

Many victims disagreed. Crowds demonstrated in the streets against what they said was an unfair betrayal. Many call for the hanging of those responsible for the toxic leak. They say the deaths were a result of poor safety procedures. They point out that tough safety standards of U.S. companies many times don't apply when the company has a plant in a foreign country. Union Carbide insists the leak was caused deliberately by an angry worker. The case may drag on for years as unhappy survivors continue to press for a better judgment.

Chapter 5

War Against Nature:
The Persian Gulf Conflict

Diary of Hammad Dosari, Iraqi Soldier
(Sunday, February 17, 1991)

The Americans are coming. Already their Cobra helicopters have fired on us. My commander has given the order to retreat; soon we'll be in our trucks heading home to Iraq. I've been guarding this oil well for months now. I am ready to go home, though I look at our retreat with bitterness. Kuwait should be a part of Iraq. Our Supreme Commander Saddam Hussein has said this. I believe him.

The Allies will have a surprise when they finally get here. For the last several weeks our oil engineers have been watching the Kuwaitis run their wells. We know exactly what to do. This morning I placed dynamite on the oil rig I am responsible for. Then I placed sandbags over the explosives to direct the blast downward. With the twist of my wrist on an electronic detonator, the dynamite exploded...boom! Flames shot into the sky, black oily smoke billowing upward over Kuwait. As I write, I look out over the desert. Hundreds of oil wells now burn. The Americans can have this wretched place of destruction.

Journal of Thomas Mathewson, Greenpeace (March 11, 1991)

I've been sent by Greenpeace, the environmental group I work for, to assess the damage to nature that Saddam Hussein's army left before retreating back to Iraq. When I stepped off the plane in Kuwait City, I smelled burning oil. A gray pall had settled over the city. Children playing in the streets wore clothes coated with a grimy black film. In the distance I could see a line of oil wells, flames spewing upward, black smoke blotting out the afternoon sun. Hospitals report many people coming in with lung problems from breathing in the smoke. Food is also poisoned. Chemicals from the fire enter the milk of cows and sheep, making it undrinkable. Crops coated with the black film must be destroyed. Wool requires chemical cleaning before it can be used.

I'm told 640 wells went up in flames; 92 others failed to ignite, but the oil from the damaged wells gushes into the desert to create new lakes of black ooze. By the end of the year, the fires should be out, the gushers capped. But by then the damage to the environment will be unthinkable.

We drove by jeep to the Burgan oil field outside Kuwait City. As we rode through the desert heat, I kept trying to think of a reason why the Iraqis would do such a monstrous thing. I could think of no good reason. There was absolutely nothing to be gained by their military. It was eco-terrorism, plain and simple. As we got closer to the oil fields, a howling invaded my ears; the roar of the burning wells raced across the desert like mad banshees riding the wind.

An oil rig burns in the Kuwaiti desert after Iraqi forces retreated in 1991.

When we finally arrived at the oil field, my first thought was that we had left Earth and were now standing on some distant, frightful planet. The sun was completely blocked out by the black clouds. Fires raged out of control. Huge lakes of oil seeped into the desert sand. In the distance I saw, silhouetted against the flames, a small herd of camels looking for clean food and water. They would soon be dead, I knew. I saw a cormorant, a water bird common in this area, struggling for life in a lake of pure oil. It lurched about, squawking feebly. It went under the oil one last time, then I never saw it again. Here and there the bodies of dead Iraqi soldiers lie next to their shattered tanks and vehicles, covered black like the landscape they created. The horror is too much.

I asked my guide why the firefighters weren't working on the burning wells nearby. He told me most of the wells were surrounded by mines that must be cleared by the military before the firefighters can even get close. It takes a long time. For now, the wells continue to burn. I saw two men in silver suits inspecting the oil-encrusted, burning sand near a fiery well. Even a hundred yards away, the fire is so intense that skin burns. It will be hard to put these horrible, flaming giants to sleep.

This afternoon my guide took me to the Persian Gulf. Even before the war the Gulf was one of the most polluted bodies of water in the world. Now it is truly a nightmare. As I stood on shore, a black tide lapped at my boots. Dead birds and other animals litter the greasy shore. During the war Iraqis blew up oil tanks, releasing the petroleum into the water. They also deliberately released oil at several terminals in the gulf, hoping to pollute the shores of Saudi Arabia to the south. They succeeded. The Coast Guard estimates four to six million barrels of oil were released, enough to coat hundreds of miles of beaches and sensitive wetlands.

Later that day, I took a helicopter to survey the damage. From the air it looked like some giant child had taken a crayon and smeared the coastline with black ugliness. Even high up in the copter, I could smell the aroma of petroleum. The Persian Gulf teems with life. Its shallow waters make it easy for sea grasses, algae and plankton to grow. These in turn support a huge variety of fish and bird populations. But the colossal spill has wiped out huge areas. And because the gulf recirculates its waters slowly, it will be years before the ecosystem recovers.

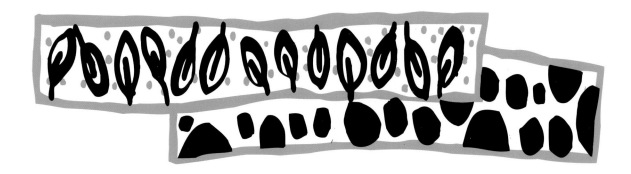

Postscript: *Two years after Operation Desert Storm, the effects of the fires and oil spills are still being felt; pools of oil have affected ground water, oil slicks have killed off fish and shrimp in their shallow-water habitats. It will be years, possibly decades, before nature heals itself. The damage to humans in the area is less certain. The fires are now out, but scientists are uncertain of the long-term effects of the toxic metals released by the fires, the oil slicks, and the explosives detonated during the war. Children are especially vulnerable. Only time will tell the lasting legacy of Saddam Hussein's war on nature.*

Chapter 6

Eastern Europe: Black Dawn

Memoir of Danko Ruse, Factory Worker, Poland (May 1991)

In the name of progress, my country poisoned the air, the land, the water; they never thought of the people who had to live in the shadows of the great soot-billowing factories. They only thought of the State and the Communist Party. Now we pay the price.

For over 50 years, until the fall of communism, we lived under a system that exploited natural resources as quickly as possible. Under orders from Moscow, huge polluting factories were built with little regard to the health of the people. The factories have few pollution-control devices like those in America and other Western counties. Our technology was out of date, but it didn't matter; we only wanted short-term gains, with no thought to environmental consequences. The results are catastrophic, and now that the Communists are gone, the truth can finally be told. In my home country of Poland, one third of our 38 million people live in "ecological hazard" zones. Half of Czechoslovakia's drinking water fails to meet the country's own health standards. In the industrialized areas of the former East Germany, half of the children have bronchitis and eczema because of the pollution. Industrial waste pollutes almost 70 percent of Bulgaria's farmland and 65 percent of its river waters. Bucharest, Romania, has no sewage-treatment plant. In most other parts of the country, sewage plants do not work.

factory spewing
black carbon

Factories like this one choked the air in Eastern Europe for
so many years that many areas are now virtually unlivable.

This is a land where school children practice putting on their face masks in case there is a sulfur dioxide alert day; where factory workers die of cancer and lung disease; where children grow sick from the toxic poisons in the food they eat, the air they breathe, the water they drink. The pollution is everywhere; it is inescapable. In Copsa Mica, Romania, black carbon falls from the nearby factories, turning everything it touches black. The trees and crops are stunted. Sheep must be washed of their black coating before the wool can be brought to market. Children playing outside grow black with soot. It is a land of eternal night.

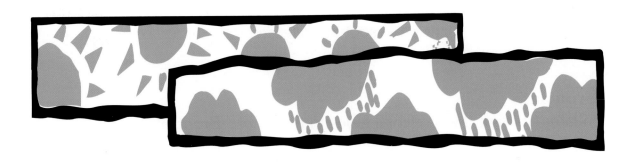

Postscript: *Since the collapse of Communism, the fresh air of freedom is beginning to blow through Eastern Europe. The former governments' policies have been disgraced. The worst factories have been shut down. (Unfortunately, this also has caused massive, short-term unemployment). The new leaders know they can no longer create factories without thought to the environment. All over Eastern Europe, governments have pledged huge cleanup efforts, and Western companies are beginning to invest in new, cleaner factories. The cleanup effort will take a long time, but for the people's sake, especially the children, they must be successful. Much is to be done. East and West must work together. It's time for the land to heal.*

Glossary

Black Carbon
Created when factories incompletely burn coal, oil, wood or other fuels. Fine black particles of soot are released into the air, covering the surrounding countryside.

Bronchitis
Inflammation of the bronchial tubes in the lungs. Bronchitis can be caused by viral or bacterial infection or by the inhalation of irritating fumes like tobacco smoke or air pollution. Symptoms include cough, fever, and chest pains.

Communism
A society in which property, particularly real property and the means of production, is held in common among all the people. Since the State (the government) is deemed to be more important than individual citizens, communist countries often create industries that use high-pollution factories without regard to the people they harm.

Crude Oil
Oil fresh out of the ground that has not yet been refined into products like gasoline or paint. It is a black, gooey, flammable liquid that occurs naturally in deposits, usually beneath the surface of the earth. Accidents that spill crude oil are very difficult to clean up.

Double Hulls

Many new oil tankers are now built with two hulls, one inside the other. If a ship with a double hull has an accident, like running aground on rocks, there is a good chance only the outer hull will be pierced. The inner hull remains intact, keeping the cargo, like crude oil, from spilling into the sea.

Ecosystem

A community of plants and animals in an environment supplying the raw materials for life, i.e., chemical elements (or food) and water. An ecosystem is defined by climate, altitude, latitude, water, and soil characteristics, and other physical conditions. When pollution enters an ecosystem, the whole balance of life can be thrown out of balance, resulting in plant and animal deaths or extinction.

Eczema

A swelling of the skin with redness, itching, and an outbreak of sores that discharge pus and become encrusted and scaly. Many times occurs because of severe industrial pollution.

Oil field

A large section of land containing oil. When oil fields are developed, many different kinds of machines are used to get at the oil, including oil drills, oil pumps, and storage tanks.

Pesticide

A biological, physical, or chemical agent used to kill plants or animals considered harmful to human beings. Unfortunately, many pesticides are also harmful to people if exposed in too great a quantity.

Petroleum

See *Crude Oil.*

Pollution-Control Devices

Devices used by oil and coal-burning industries to reduce the amount of pollution released into the air, especially soot. *See Black Carbon.*

Radiation

Tiny particles of matter or invisible rays that can damage living things. While radiation is all around us, such as in the form of sunlight or in some rocks (background radiation), the waste from nuclear reactors is of special concern because of how concentrated the radiation is. Severe radiation poisoning, such as from a leak or explosion from a nuclear power plant, can include weakness, loss of appetite, vomiting, diarrhea, bleeding, increased chance of infection, and—if severe enough—brain damage and death. Even in small doses radiation can be hazardous because of long-term genetic effects.

Skimmers

Boats that skim over oil spills, scooping up oil on the surface using booms and other oil-absorbing devices.

Sulfur dioxide

A colorless, extremely irritating gas or liquid, used in many industrial processes, especially the manufacture of sulfuric acid.

Supertanker

Huge ships that can carry millions of gallons of oil or other cargo.

Valve

A device that controls the flow of gases, liquids, or loose materials through structures like pipes. In Bhopal, India, a faulty valve may have been the cause of the release of toxic gas into the air, resulting in the deaths of hundreds of people.

Index

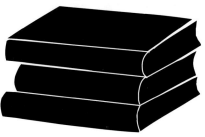

TARGET EARTH™ COMMITMENT

At Target, we're committed to the environment. We show this commitment not only through our own internal efforts but also through the programs we sponsor in the communities where we do business.

Our commitment to children and the environment began when we became the Founding International Sponsor for Kids for Saving Earth, a non-profit environmental organization for kids. We helped launch the program in 1989 and supported its growth to three-quarters of a million club members in just three years.

Our commitment to children's environmental education led to the development of an environmental curriculum called Target Earth™, aimed at getting kids involved in their education and in their world.

In addition, we worked with Abdo & Daughters Publishing to develop the Target Earth™ Earthmobile, an environmental science library on wheels that can be used in libraries, or rolled from classroom to classroom.

Target believes that the children are our future and the future of our planet. Through education, they will save the world!

TARGET®

Minneapolis-based Target Stores is an upscale discount department store chain of 517 stores in 33 states coast-to-coast, and is the largest division of Dayton Hudson Corporation, one of the nation's leading retailers.